Roosters as Pets

A Care Guide for Pet Roosters

Rooster Breed General Info, Purchasing, Care, Cost, Keeping, Health, Supplies, Food, Breeding and More Included!

By Lolly Brown

Foreword

If you're looking for a different kind of pet to keep, then a rooster might work well for you! Roosters don't just fly (in a way), they also crow – and for a good purpose. They are, in fact, have more abilities than flying birds and other household pets alike! They can function as pets, as an 'alarm clock,' as a guard to guide and protect your other chicks/chickens against potential predators including burglars in your house, and can also brought forth many mini – rooster breeds for you and your hens!

Throughout history and until today, roosters are always portrayed as a fowl who crows during the break of dawn. Although people's concept of roosters are not exactly true, many people today especially those living in rural areas or farms that are far from the metropolis are still relying on the rooster's crows to wake them up each morning, and start the day right.

This book will cover everything you need to know about how to raise roosters in your backyard or your farm, how you can keep a good poultry, the origin and history of roosters, and the basics of keeping roosters as pets!

Cock-a-doodle-doo!

Table of Contents

Introduction

Also known as cocks or cockerels back in the older times, rooster is a male chicken/ gallinaceous bird with a scientific name of *Gallus gallus*. The male chicken was originally coined "rooster" in USA, and the term was also widely used in Canada, New Zealand, Australia, and other parts of the world. Its older names which denotes a young chicken or a bird was used mostly in Europe during the early days particularly in the UK and Ireland.

Perhaps the most distinct feature or best characteristic of roosters is that they crow! Hens (female chicken) can also crow but not as much as roosters do, and oftentimes hens really don't. In fact, you can already identify which ones are the roosters because they already start crowing as early as 3 months, and their hackles also start developing along with their crowing abilities.

A rooster's temperament and behavioral characteristic or personality can be differentiated in the way they crow and also how often they do it in a day. You'll soon realize, especially if you're going to take care lots of rooster, that they have their own distinct voices and patterns of crowing. Some roosters are quite vociferous or very vocal, you'll hear them crow more than a few times a day, while some only do it at certain times. These birds also crow if they are threatened, if they are proclaiming a territory from other species, if they are trying to attract a mate, or even if there are burglars around the house!

Roosters have other crowing calls as well, and they can also cluck just like their female counterparts, but they don't do it as much compared to hens. You'll oftentimes find them just sitting on a slightly high post or fence during the day, where they can overlook their territory and serve as the guard for the group. Roosters will do a distinct alarm call to alert other chickens that a potential threat or predator is near its surrounding territories, and if it is indeed a threat, he will crow or attack it.

Throughout history and until today, roosters are always portrayed as a fowl who crows during the break of dawn. They also served as the 'alarm clock' especially for early risers back in the day. However, this idea is somewhat inaccurate simply because roosters can crow anytime they want, and of course they don't have a sense of time. Although people's concept of roosters are not exactly true, many people today especially those living in rural areas or farms that are far from the metropolis are still relying on the rooster's crows to wake them up each morning, and start the day right.

Chapter One: The Rooster Species and Historical Significance

Roosters are classified as domestic chickens or birds that cannot fly. There are about 150 chicken breeds that differ in sizes, colors, and personalities. Such fowls were believed to have descended from an Indian and Asian ancestor like the Red Jungle fowl. There are actually more chickens existing in the world today than humans and other bird species alike! These fowls have been the most useful bird species throughout human history.

In fact, they even have a historical significance in almost all the major religions since the early days. Aside from being a source of food and a crower, roosters in particular are also used in cockfights in some parts of the world, and the best part is that you can keep them as household pets! This chapter will give you the biological information about roosters including its taxonomy, appearance, and types as well as its religious significance.

Taxonomy

Roosters (and hens alike) have a scientific name of *Gallus gallus*. They belong in Kingdom *Animalia*, Phylum *Chordata*, Class *Aves*, Order *Galliformes*, Family Phasianidae, Genus *Gallus*, and Species *Gallus gallus*.

Origin and Distribution

Roosters are native in the forests of India as well as Southeast Asia. Scientists believed that this fowl species occurred about 7,000 years ago, and it's mostly distributed in different countries in Asia such as India, Philippines, China, Indonesia, Malaysia, Burma and the likes. The closest relatives of roosters and domestic chickens are wild fowl species like the Burmese Red Jungle Fowl, Indian Red Jungle Fowl, and Gray Jungle Fowl.

The art of egg coloring and artificial chicken are believed to have come from ancient Egypt and China, and although the practice was lost as time goes by, the art of hatching re – emerged around the 18th century.

Physical and Behavioral Characteristics of Roosters

The sizes of roosters greatly vary according to its breed. On average domestic rooster chickens weighs about 8 ½ pounds (around 3 kg), has a length of 25 to 40 centimeters, and its wings measures about 60 to 90 centimeters.

Physical Features of Roosters

- Has a striking plumage compared to hens
- Usually has pointed and brightly colored feathers on their tails and necks (though color patterns vary)
- Roosters are significantly heavier and larger than hens
- The rooster's body color is generally brighter and vibrant than hens
- Roosters likes to crow loud and long, they can also chuckle like hens
- The crowing sound is a territorial sign for roosters
- They cannot produce or lay eggs since they are the male species

- The average lifespan of a rooster is 5 to 7 years but there have been instances where they live for more than 10 years.

Behavioral/Territorial Characteristics of Roosters

- Some roosters can tend to have aggressive behaviors depending on the breed and individual personality
- Aside from being a meat source, they also serve as players during cockfights which are legal in some countries.
- Roosters and chickens in general are flightless fowls; they do tend to flap their wings and attempt to fly but only for a short distance and a limited height.
- Roosters can only fly a maximum of about 4 feet, but they cannot stay in the air like birds.
- If they encounter a predator, they will run and also attempt to fly for a while.
- Roosters and chickens are communal species, which means that they like it best if they live with the same species as them or if they are with their flock.
- Some roosters will tend to dominate other chicken species to establish a so – called pecking order; once such dominant roosters are removed, there will be a disruption in the pecking order, and a new one will be established among the chicken breeds.

- Dominant roosters may have priority especially when accessing food and the nests.

Other General Rooster Information

- Roosters and chicken are omnivores; they usually eat vegetables such as herbs, grubs, leaves, and chicken feeds, and grains. For their meat diet they like to eat small and large insects sometimes even the larva, small mammals such as mice, and other meat source. Gizzard is an organ in their stomachs that process foods.

- Roosters have a particular courting and mating ritual. Oftentimes, if they find a hen they want to mate with, they crow and call other chickens to eat first. When a female chicken is already familiar with the crow of a rooster, they may eventually mate.

- The usual predators of roosters particularly if they are in the wild includes fox, snake, owls, eagles, hawks, opossums, raccoons, bobcats, skunks, and other reptile or mammal species larger than the rooster.

Types of Roosters

Roosters have different breeds per country; the size, temperament, nature, and physical characteristics greatly vary around the world but they are generally classified into groups, and raised for the same purpose. Usually people take care of roosters because of its meat quality, and for the purposes of fertilizing the eggs of a hen especially if they are running a poultry business. But there are some people (like you) who may want to keep these beautiful birds and raise them as pets. Below are some types of roosters in major countries and continents around the world. These are only a brief overview of the roosters that may be available in your country, and could be suitable for your flock (if you already have one).

American Roosters

There are about a hundred breeds of roosters in the United States alone. Such roosters were bred in the country, and some were even named after the states in which they were developed. The most historically renowned rooster species is called the Barred Plymouth Rock because it is the standard of perfection in America since 1874. It is known as the most distinct rooster breed, and also has a reputation for being the most docile rooster breed in America. Such roosters are popular for backyard raising. Other American roosters include but are not limited to the following:

- White Plymouth Rock Rooster
- Iowa Blue Rooster
- California Gray Rooster
- Rhode Island Red Rooster
- Delaware Rooster
- New Hampshire Rooster

European Roosters

There are also lots of different rooster breeds that were developed in Europe. The most popular rooster breed is called the Buff Orpington Rooster, also known as Golden Beauties, which was developed from the United Kingdom. Aside from its docile temperament, Europeans love the Buff Orpington Rooster's juicy meat and their beautiful plump. Here are the other breeds of rooster that are popular in Europe:

- Altsteirers Roosters (Belgium)
- Sulmtaler (Austria)
- East Frisian Gulls (Germany)
- Old English Games Rooster (UK)

- Polish Rooster
- Bergischer Long Crowers (Germany)
- Marsh Daisies (UK)
- Frizzle Fowl (UK)

Asian Roosters

Aside from Western developed roosters, many breeds are also available in other countries in Asia. Such rooster breeds have their own set of characteristics and temperament, one popular Asian rooster breed is called a Chinese Silkie Rooster, which was known for its reputation of being the best medicinal food in China as its meat helps prevent diabetes, anemia, and other diseases. There are also other local breeds in other Asian countries like India and Chile that are distinct in their own ways. In the Philippines, roosters are used for cockfights where people can bet and gamble their money on a particular rooster, though the government has already deemed the game as illegal in most states.

Hybrid Roosters

There are also species that are called as hybrid roosters because they were developed through crossbreeding a purebred rooster to another hybrid rooster. You can try to get these kinds of breeds if it's available around your area. Such hybrid roosters have many advantages compared to a purebred rooster; the meats are usually high quality, such roosters can also fertilize more eggs, and can survive in cold environments. Here are some of the popular hybrid roosters you might want to consider in keeping as pets:

- Red Sex Link Roosters
- Black Sex Link Roosters
- Crossbreeds of Rhode Island Red and Delaware Rooster
- Cinnamon Queens Roosters
- Cherry Eggers Roosters
- Crossbreeds of Rhode Island Red and Barred Rock Rooster

Historical and Religious Significance

Roosters are considered a sacred animal in many cultures and in different religions all over the world since ancient times. This unique fowl species is embedded in various belief systems, and it is also the animal that is mostly offered to gods during religious worship or sacred rituals. This section will give you an overview of the religious significance of the rooster species throughout history.

Animism and Shamanism

Anito

Roosters are considered as traditional animal spirits especially in Southeast Asian countries particularly in the Philippines; roosters are called *Anito*. Roosters are part of Filipinos' indigenous beliefs, and it is usually the animal being offered to honor the local gods and deities. As previously mentioned roosters are also used in cockfights specifically in northern Philippine provinces. Before cockfights became a gambling game for locals, it is a form of fertility worship, and is practiced by traditional Filipino Christians during the early times.

Aluk to Dolo

In Indonesia, a sect religion called Agama Hindu Dharma also incorporates a rooster in some of their religious rituals particularly when doing the funeral ceremonies. They held a sacred cockfight during such ceremonies, and it is believed that this ritual can revive a dead person, or grants a wish.

Kaharingan

This is a folk religion in Indonesia that is considered as part of Animist Hinduism. Such religion believes that humans are the 'fighting cocks' of the gods, and that cockfighting and the rooster itself is introduced by these gods. The rooster is also being waved during sacred rituals before presenting it to the gods; it also involves the rooster's blood as part of the sacrificial offering so that the gods will bless the people and also guide them in their lives.

Other religions that include roosters as part of sacred rituals and sacrificial offerings are Ikenga (Nigeria), Miao (China), and Santeria (Cuba), and Imbolc fests (Celtic, Neo – Druidry, Neo – Paganism) among others.

Buddhism

In Buddhism, the walls of the temple usually depict roosters in a cockfight, and it's also a part of the Songkran Festival held in the Three Pagodas Pass religious site. There are also many Buddhist temples particularly in Thailand that depicts Buddha holding a rooster and is in a fighting stance. However, in some Tibetan Buddhist murals, roosters symbolize greed. Some people are debating whether or not a rooster is still considered a sacred animal today.

Hinduism

God of War called Karthikeya was believed to have a rooster depicted in his flag. Other Hindu deities like Theyyam gods, and Ida Ratu Saung are also seen holding a rooster while blood is being spilled. The blood spilling is represents the purification of evil spirits. Other forms of Hinduism and Hindu practices like Balinese Hinduism, Pongal, and Tulunadu also use roosters to perform sacred religious rites such as blood offerings and cockfighting.

Judaism

In Judaism, roosters are part of celestial manifestations. According to rabbi literature, the crows of a rooster are also the general marking the time; the crowing also means summoning of priests and Israelites. The act of cockfighting is also interpreted as a religious vessel particularly in a Jewish rituals called Kapparos; the rooster was worn and swung around the head as part of the sacrificial practice before the Day of Atonement or Yom Kippur. It's also an emblem that was believed to have been carried by the residents of Caria.

Christianity

In Indonesia and the Philippines, two of the only Christian countries in Southeast Asia, the rooster are also a religious vessel during the ancient times. In Indonesia, cocks or roosters are usually carved in catacombs of ancient Christian religious figures. The rooster also represents immortality, resurrection, and victory over death. Roosters can also be found in canonical gospels in the bible, and several basilicas. Pope Gregory I also said that the rooster is the suitable emblem of Christianity.

Islam

In the Islam religion, roosters signals the spiritual endowment of Allah because according to one of the hadith collections called Sunni Islam, whenever the roosters crow, people should ask for the blessing of Allah "for they have seen an angel."

Chapter Two: Keeping Roosters as Pets

This chapter will focus on how to take care and properly keep roosters. Just like any household pets, you need to ensure that you can provide for its needs – both its basic needs, and the environmental needs – before you purchase a rooster so that your pet can live adequately and happily. You'll get to learn the permits you may need to acquire, the pros and cons of keeping roosters, how to introduce it to your other pets particularly if you have an existing flock, and the basic costs of keeping a rooster. These are the things you need to consider before you make the decision of purchasing a rooster or two!

Do You Need a Permit?

Keeping roosters is subject to some laws and regulations that are usually quite complicated depending on the city or state you live in. In the USA, the ordinances and local laws greatly vary, and no towns are identical when it comes to the requirements that you need to present to get a poultry permit (even if you don't plan of keeping many roosters or maintaining a poultry). It is therefore highly recommended that you first learn about the city ordinances or regulations in your local municipality so that you'll have an idea on what it takes to keep roosters legally. Below is a quick guideline of what you need to do in order to know the rules in your respective areas:

- **Know your jurisdiction.** Make sure to know the municipality, town or your area of residence.

- **Inquire in your local government about the regulations regarding poultry keeping.** You need to go to the office or contact your local government about the laws or permits you need to acquire for you to be able to keep a rooster or poultry in your home. You can head to the information desk or speak to a government employee in charge of the local laws regarding livestock.

- **Search online regarding the laws.** If you don't have time to go directly to your local government, you can also check online if they have a website, and if there's information there about livestock regulations. If you are unsure or the regulations are quite confusing, you can probably find a number where you can call and talk to the local animal control officer or anyone who can assist you.

- **Visit your local courthouse** (for residents residing in remote areas). If you're not living in a city or town, then the best option for you is to go to the nearest courthouse, and ask about the local laws. You may also view a database online, if you can find one, and check if your area, municipality or town is listed in it.

- **Talk to your local associations or subdivision organizations.** If you live in a subdivision, there may be a new set of laws or regulations you need to follow, which is why it's best that you go talk to the head of the local associations within your subdivision or village. However, sometimes no one is particularly enforcing anything as long as you don't get complaints about your chickens or roosters but of course it's still better to ask local officers to make sure you're not breaking any laws, and get the necessary permits if need be.

Rooster Regulations You May Encounter

Here are the regulations and restrictions you may encounter when keeping a rooster or poultry. Keep in mind that not all of it will apply to you, check your local towns for confirmation:

- **Licensing/Permit Fees** – before you get a permit or license, most towns and municipalities will require that you pay a fee aside from the requirements/documents you may need to pass. However, some towns may not charge you of anything as long as the number of cocks you keep will not exceed depending on what is set in the regulation.

- **Number of Birds You Can Legally Keep** – Some towns have a limit as to how many roosters you can keep in your house or property while some cities don't have that kind of rule. If ever your town have a bird count limit, then it is best that you follow that otherwise you may be fined or have a penalty for each bird that will exceed. Sometimes the property or space size is the determining factor as to how many fowls you can keep. Most towns, however, have already a specific number; usually 3 to 4 fowls are only permitted in one property. Check if your towns or municipality is flexible regarding the bird limit.

- **Rooster Regulations**

  Some municipalities have strict regulations for roosters since they can be quite noisy. Sometimes a rooster is only allowed if it's 4 months and below. Generally, hens are more acceptable since they're use for egg production. Check your area if they'll allow you to keep a rooster, and know the conditions you need to follow.

- **Housing Requirements**

  There are towns that have a set of requirements when it comes to housing your roosters. Some areas don't allow free running of chickens even if they're in your backyard, while other towns need to approve first the materials you're going to use for the rooster enclosure.

- **Public Concerns**

  You may also encounter rules that can raise concern around your neighborhood such as the smell, noise, health concerns of chickens that can affect people, cleanliness, proper manure disposal etc. You definitely will encounter these nuisances so make sure you know it.

- **Rooster Slaughtering**

  Some towns allow slaughtering, some don't. Sometimes the rules are unclear especially in subdivisions or residential areas. Make sure to ask proper authorities regarding this so that you won't get complaints or be subject to restrictions.

- **Special Regulations**

  You may also encounter some kind of special regulations depending on where you live or the property where you're roosters or poultry is being housed. Here are some examples of special regulations that could be in place:

  - Chicken feeds should be placed in sealed containers that are animal proof.
  - The chicken regulations are subject to a one year trial, and there'll be a yearly evaluation.
  - 1 chicken is permitted to the set minimum for every additional 1,000 sq. feet of land.
  - Roosters and hens are allowed in areas that are multi – zoned.
  - The coops should be mobile in order to prevent waste and bacteria build up.

Pros and Cons of Keeping a Rooster

Before you purchase a rooster chick, make sure that you have weighed the pros and cons of keeping one. This section will give you an overview of the things you need to consider:

Pros

- Roosters are colorful fowl species
- They're the ones that can fertilize hens making sure that egg production and supply is on – going.
- Roosters function as guards of the flock. They protect and defend the flock against predators
- When roosters find a food source, he usually alerts other roosters or chickens about it. Oftentimes, he'll let other chickens eat first before partaking.
- Roosters loves treats, and can also be taught some tricks
- They usually like to be petted and even complimented
- They crow anytime they want, so if you'd like to hear that kind of sound especially during the morning, it can make you feel good especially if you wanted to have a rural ambience in your home

- Roosters can also alert you if a potential burglar or stranger is lurking outside your house/property.
- They also function as insect controllers because they love to eat unwanted pests in your backyard.
- They can also bond with the family

Cons

- Roosters crow almost all the time, you can get disturbed by it, and you can also get noise complaints from your neighbors
- Keeping roosters may require you to follow lots of regulations
- You'll most likely need to get a permit before you can keep one which can be an additional expense
- You may need to work out the permits/licenses and talk to certain officials which can also be time consuming especially if you are a busy person
- Your hens (if you keep some) will not be injured by the rooster's beak during mating
- Sometimes roosters can be aggressive
- You don't need to worry about a rooster jumping at people or dominating your hen collection
- May not be suitable for keepers with very young children or those with allergies as their feathers can cause allergic reactions.

Rooster Introduction

This section will cover how you can introduce a new rooster to your existing flock of hens, and a flock with existing roosters. You need to make sure that the ratio of roosters within a flock (either with hens or with other roosters) is just right to avoid domination and aggressiveness. Obviously, if you don't have an existing flock of chickens you won't have any problem with this. However, if you do keep other animals like cats or dogs, you need to make sure that they have separate spaces, and that your roosters are housed in enclosures or coops that your household pets can't access to avoid injuries and predation.

Rooster Introduction to a Flock of Hens

If you have an existing hen collection, and you wanted to introduce a rooster for the first time, you just need to isolate the rooster for about a month just like isolating a bird. You can place him in an open enclosure or fence where the hens can see him and meet him. After a day or two, you can release the rooster into your flock of hens. Make sure that you provide a substantial amount of food for your flock to avoid competition.

You'll soon notice that the new rooster will easily get along with your hens, and will flirt around them. He will find food for them, protect them, and gather them at sunset. You'll have no problem introducing a male chicken to your set of hens. You can expect to have an ongoing supply of eggs in no time!

Rooster Introduction to a Flock with Existing Roosters

Introducing a new rooster to your flock wherein one or more roosters are already present can be a little bit tricky. It can spell trouble for you and for your other roosters as well as hens. You need to take precaution because if roosters are together, you can expect cockfights and bloodshed.

Make sure that every time you introduce a new rooster, you first isolate him but include around 6 to 12 hens before you release them all in your existing flock. The isolated rooster and his own set of hens should be isolated in an enclosure with enough space to roam around, but can also be seen and met with the other roosters and hens in your flock, so that they can recognize that the new rooster came with his own set of established flock. If this is not done, the old rooster will become aggressive towards the new rooster because he already claimed the flock. You may still see a few scratches even after isolating your new rooster with his own hens but it there'll be fewer cockfights.

The amount of space or property should also be more than enough to accommodate your flock as it can make a difference with how your existing flock will react if you introduce another rooster. Roosters are territorial animals, so to avoid cockfights when a rooster goes into another "rooster's territory" make sure that the space is more than enough, otherwise they can get aggressive and competitive with one another. Avoid overcrowding as well. If you don't have that much space, then ensure that the roosters have their own coops or pen.

If you happen to own an aggressive rooster, make sure that he is have his own pen (preferably with a roof) and his own set of hens to avoid flying to another rooster's space or stealing other rooster's hens. Usually, there'll be a rooster leader within the flock, if it's already established, the 'weak' rooster will back down and let the strong one dominate.

If you acquire a rooster chick, and raised them together, chances are they will spar with one another at an early age, and the more they grow, the bloodier it gets especially when they start developing spurs/beaks. If you don't provide them with enough hens for their own, they'll most likely kill each other even if they grew up together. They can also form a relationship once the dominant rooster is established. The dominant one will serve as the leader of the flock while the weak one will just back down and wait for a hen that's separated from the flock. If ever the dominant rooster caught the weak rooster mating with one of his hens, he will attack and can even kill the weak one so make sure that they have their own sets to avoid such circumstances.

Costs of Keeping a Rooster

This section will provide you with a breakdown of the possible ongoing costs you'll entail once you decide to keep one or more roosters. Generally, the cost of keeping a hen and a rooster is the same, the prices will only vary depending on the age of the chick, the breed, the city/state where you bought it, the fees of the permits you need to acquire, the materials (for enclosures), the possible medical/vet expenses, and the brands of the food/ toys you want to buy for your pet.

Purchase Price

Generally, a rooster chick costs between $3 and $50. This depends on the breed of the rooster, the age, the medical expenses incurred by the owner, and the likes. The prices will vary from one state to another, so feel free to do some research on where you can find the best quality chicks at a reasonable price and raised by a reputable breeder.

It's better to buy small male chicks instead of acquiring an older one or a fully matured rooster, the downside of course is that you may need to wait for a few months before you can buy a hatchling. Ordinary roosters can cost around $3 to $5 while hybrid roosters and popular breeds can cost $30 to $50 and above per chick. A rooster pullet (juvenile rooster) may cost you around $20 and above. If you want to save money, and you're not that concern with the quality of the breed, you can choose to adopt a rooster for free! Just look for a rooster adoption ads or talk to breeders who may have unwanted roosters.

Housing Expenses

The coop for your rooster (for chicks and matured ones) on average costs $500. If you're going to buy one from fancy stores or something made out of quality and durable materials, expect to pay around $1,000 to $4,000. Secondhand coops are usually cheaper, you can buy one for just $50 or more. Most keepers just build their own coops or enclosures to save money. Sometimes it's made out of recycled materials, and cheap alternatives. If you want to improvise make sure you have the proper hand tools to aid you.

If you wanted to raise male chicks, then you'll need a brooder. You can buy a ready-made brooder for about $75 and up. Again, you can just build your own brooder for your small chicks; the materials that keepers usually use to improvise are Rubbermaid tubs, old packing cases, crates and the likes. Just make sure that there's enough space for each chick. The hatchlings will stay there for around 6 weeks before being moved to a coop. You'll also need a light bulb and heat lamp to keep the hatchlings warm which can cost you around $20 - $30.

Feeders, Bedding, and Toys

Feeders including water systems for the coop usually costs $8 to $40, of course this will again depend on the brand, design, and size. Some keepers improvise the feeders by just making egg boxes as feeders, while a shallow dish to place water can also work if the male chicks are still young.

When it comes to bedding, you can provide your pet with wood shavings, straws, or sawdust pellets that usually costs from $3 to $12 per 40 pounds of bag (for sawdust pellets).

When it comes to toys, you can keep your roosters entertained by buying different chicken toys that are usually available in pet stores or online suppliers. If you want to save money, you can get creative and just opt to create a DIY (Do – It – Yourself) toy materials to entertain your chicks/roosters.

Food Expenses

For chicks, you can buy a 50 pound bag that will cost around $15 to $20 depending on the quality, brands, and if it is organic, regular, or medicated/ non – medicated. You can save money if you buy in large amounts. For juveniles and older roosters, a 50 pound bag may cost you around $18, while pellets cost between $15 and $30. Scratch grains usually costs $10 per 50 pounds.

Miscellaneous Expenses

It's best to set aside $10 to $100 per month for other expenses like medicine, neuter/caponize, vaccines, pest control, permits etc. You may need to also set aside money for vet expenses if ever your rooster gets ill.

Chapter Three: How to Purchase and Select a Healthy Rooster

By this time, you are now decided that rooster keeping is for you. You find roosters an enticing pet to take care of or to simply do the job of fertilizing your hens so that you can have your own supply of eggs. Perhaps you need it for business or you're just simply fond of keeping these beautiful fowls, whatever your reason is and your purpose of owning a rooster, it's always best that you know where to purchase it, and how to select the healthiest breed you can possibly get. A healthy rooster can mean a healthy supply of eggs and chicks which is why considering where to get it and learning how to select the best is essential as a keeper and a potential breeder.

This chapter will provide you with information on how you can find the right breeder, the qualities to look for in a chick, and the tips on how to purchase a healthy breed. You'll also be given a list of recommended websites where you can find chick or rooster breeders online as well as some guideline questions before acquiring a chick from a breeder.

Where to Purchase Roosters

You can buy fully matured roosters, and also chicks from several sources. It is important to note however, that it's much better if you buy a chick or a hatchling than a fully matured rooster, simply because it'll be easier if you're the one who's going to raise it. You'll be your own breeder in a way, and you'll learn how to raise a rooster or even a hen for that matter, properly. You'll get a chance to truly be a keeper because you're going to witness how quickly it grows, the changes in its physical appearance, and its temperament. You'll be sure that your chicken will get the best food and environment as well as the best possible medical treatment if need be. Before purchasing a chick and selecting a healthy breed, you should first learn where to acquire them which will be covered in this section.

Farm Stores

You can buy your male chick or rooster from farm stores; many people are acquiring a rooster species here because this is perhaps the most accessible and inexpensive way of getting a rooster. There could be several farm stores around your neighborhood as well especially if you're living in rural areas, which mean that you can have lots of options. However, farm stores are like pet stores for other household pets such as cats, dogs, and birds; this means that there's a big possibility that the chicks being sold here are not of great quality for many reasons. Here are some of the disadvantages in buying from farm stores:

- The chicks are usually unsexed. This is bad especially if you're just really planning to acquire a rooster and not a hen. The store owners most of the time, do not know if a chick is a male or female because it's only being delivered to them by their suppliers.

- Chicks from farm stores are generally very prone to germs and illnesses because it is exposed with other breeds of animals, you don't know how the owners are taking care of these animals, and you're not sure if they are following proper husbandry practices. The animals can also be stressed out due to the environment.

- Lastly, the owner (since they're usually not the breeder) do not know if the chicks are vaccinated or not, or may not have enough medical information about the health of the chick and how it was raised. Health is not usually guaranteed.

Chick Hatchery

Another option where you can acquire a chick is buying directly from a hatchery. The main advantage is that you can order hatchlings and even eggs (that will be ready to hatch) if you want, you'll just be the one to hatch it. You can also request for the chicks to be vaccinated against common bird illnesses like Mareks disease. You can also pick from the different breeds of roosters that are available. Unlike buying from farm stores, you are guaranteed that what you're getting is a male chick or a rooster breed. However, there are also disadvantages in acquiring a rooster from hatcheries. One of which is that usually these hatcheries are killing unwanted roosters at day one. It's mostly an ethical reason but still worth checking out if the hatchery is doing it, for some people this is not a good sign that they're reputable breeders.

Most hatcheries produce a utility stock, and not heritage breeds, if you like to purchase rare breeds then you're better off finding a backyard breeder because you're not going to find one from hatcheries.

Hatcheries are a good source of chicks if you're not after hybrid roosters or rare species. Aside from being an inexpensive option, you are guaranteed that the chick is a rooster breed, you have many options of ordinary rooster breeds to choose from depending on the availability, and you can also somewhat guarantee its health.

Private/Backyard Breeders

Buying male chicks or even fully – matured roosters from private breeders are the best option for chicken keepers especially for newbies. This is because reputable breeders are passionate about raising chickens, and majority of them put a lot of work and effort in raising a quality breeding stock. Of course, the main downside is that you'll most likely pay more than the average but just consider it a worthy investment especially if you're planning to acquire rare rooster breeds.

Another major advantage is that these reputable breeders will happily teach you how to keep such pets, how to raise them properly, how to care for it if ever it gets sick, and also give you recommendations for food brands, housing/ coop enclosures, medical matters, and lots of guidelines. These breeders will show you the ropes on how you can be a good and reputable chicken breeder yourself.

Aside from all of the perks mentioned above, you can guarantee that the chick is of top quality because you have the chance of interviewing the one who rear them, you can even request to tour around their breeding facilities so that you can be sure that the chicks, their mothers, and other breeds are housed adequately. The breeder can also give you the health history of the chick/s, and you can even ask for referrals from previous buyers for you to know if the breeder is truly reputable. Usually what newbie keepers do is search online or look for people who are passionate about chicken breeding, this is where they get recommendations of where you can buy the best chicken breeds.

Adoption for Unwanted Roosters

If you're not after the quality of the breed or you're not going to use your rooster for hatching purposes, then it's probably best that you go check adoption centers. There are many roosters out there (both older chicks and matured ones) that are abandoned by their owners. You can usually get it for free, some towns may charge you for a fee but it will be less compared to when you buy one.

The main disadvantage of course is that you don't know exactly where these roosters came from and how they were raised. Just be sure to check for any signs of illness in their body, and see if the chicken is active and not lethargic.

Guidelines before Purchasing a Rooster

These are some questions you need to ask a breeder before buying a chick. This mostly applies to backyard/private breeders but you can also ask these questions to the owners of the hatcheries or farm stores, this is one way of knowing if they are reputable breeders.

- **What rooster breeds are available?**
  Majority of chicken breeders specialize in just raising a few breeds for both economical and quality reasons. It's usually a good sign if the breeder only has a few quality rooster species because that's a sign that he/she is only selecting the best stock. Make sure that you know what kind of rooster breed you're looking for.

- **Can I purchase sexed chickens?**
  If you wanted to just purchase a rooster breed, then this is important because otherwise you might get a

hen. Most private breeders are selling sexed chicks already so you're most likely guaranteed that what you'll be getting is a male chicken. Some breeders also sell pullets (chicks that are less than a year old) and even hatchlings.

- **Is the breeder NPIP (National Poultry Improvement Plan) Certified?**
  This is not a requirement but it's a plus point if the breeder you chose is NPIP certified or that his/her breeds are certified by this organization. This only means that the breeding stocks are tested for diseases and have passed. This is a guarantee to you as the buyer that the flocks are all healthy and not carrying any kinds of chicken diseases.

- **What is the heritage of the roosters?**
  If you're the type of person who wanted 'show birds' (rooster breeds that are qualified to join a showing competition) then make sure that your rooster is acquired from a private breeder. The heritage of the rooster will tell you if the rooster is show quality and not just utility kinds of birds. You'll obviously have to pay premium for such birds so make sure that the heritage/ bird lineage is the one you like, and if it's a rooster that has been shown before. Keeping a rooster for showing purposes will take lots of commitment on

your part! Make sure that you have the time and money in maintaining the health and physical condition of your rooster. In the next few chapters, you'll get to learn everything about showing birds.

- **How old is the chick?**

  The age of the chick can affect the price you have to pay. The older the chicks, the higher the price because they required more care.

- **What's the personality of the rooster breed?**

  This is something you can ask the breeder about because each breed of roosters has different temperament. There are those that are more aggressive (can be perfect for cockfighting), and there are those that are placid which are perfect as pets or for showing purposes. You don't want to acquire a generally aggressive rooster breed especially if you have other roosters in your flock unless you want a cockfight and chaos in your backyard.

- **Is the chick or rooster vaccinated already?**

  You have to know what vaccines have already been given, and you also have to get the certification from the breeder because you'll also need it as proof when you get a permit or license for your rooster.

- **What are the environmental restrictions for the specific rooster breed?**

  There are certain rooster breeds (especially those rare breeds) that require extra care and may only be advisable for certain places. Some birds are not best in places where the ground is too muddy or too wet, while other breeds cannot be acclimated in extreme weather conditions. Make sure to consider your environmental conditions to see if the rooster breed can adequately live in your area.

- **What do they feed on?**

  Majority of breeders, especially reputable ones, will advise you to continue giving the chicken feeds that they fed while they're raising the chicks. If you wish to change the chick's diet, then it's best to ask the breeder on how to do it. Usually, they'll tell you to continue giving the same feeds until the chicks reach a certain age before slowly transitioning to a new one. You'll also have to know if the feed is medicated or has coccidiostat; if the feeds are medicated that means that the chicks have not yet been vaccinated against coccidiosis disease.

- **Is your place safe from predators?**

  This is obviously a question for you as the future keeper. You need to ensure that your flock is secured and protected against potential threats like snakes, hawks, and the likes. It's also important to note that there are certain rooster breeds that prefer to roost in trees and do not like to stay in coops, this is not advisable if there'll be potential threats at night in your area, or if you live in a residential area.

- **Is the breed suitable for you?**
  Another thing you need to consider is if the rooster breed you'll choose is either friendly or flighty. There are breeds that doesn't like to be petted, and there are breeds that can be perfect for kids (at least while the male chicks are still quite young), and there are also several breeds that are easy to handle and not that aggressive which can be perfect for beginners.

Signs of a Healthy Chick

Here are the things to look out for when picking out the right male chick to keep as a pet:

- Make sure that there's no eye discharge. The eyes of the chick should be shiny and also clear. The eyelids should not be swelling, and shouldn't be protruding.

- The nostrils should be clear with no discharge, and should be open as well.

- The chick/rooster should be able to breathe even if their mouths are closed (except during hot climate). If the bird is breathing with its mouth open, it's most likely ill.

- The wings of the rooster should not look twisted. Some breeds have wings that are pointed downwards, while most are carried close to its body. The important thing is that it's not droop, damaged or has any sort of abnormalities because it can affect its offspring if it's genetic.

- The feathers should not have huge patches, and there shouldn't be any sign of swelling or sore skin. The feathers should be smooth as well. There are times when the tail feathers are pulled out, but if the rooster's skin appears to be intact and the feathers are not fluffed otherwise the bird may be ill.

- The feet of the rooster and hens alike shouldn't turn outward, the toes should also be straightly pointed, and the hock joints shouldn't touch, same with the toes. The feet shouldn't be webbed (like in ducks) otherwise that can mean that there's a genetic problem or abnormality. The legs and the bottom of the foot shouldn't be swelling and the skin shouldn't have any sign of soreness.

- The rectal area (vent) shouldn't have any wounds, and shouldn't be matted with feces.

- The chick should be active and alert. If the chick appears lethargic, and can be easily handled it might be ill. You want chicks that slightly avoid strangers and those that love to chuckle and play around.

- During the day the chicks are usually active, while during warm climates most chicks are usually less active. Some are flighty while some are calm, so make sure that you know the general temperament of the breed you like. See if the characteristic both physically and behaviorally will match the chicks you chose from the flock.

Chapter Four: Coops and Enclosures for Roosters

This chapter will focus on the overview of the kind of housing or coop enclosure you need to provide for your rooster and chickens alike. Proper housing will ensure that your roosters will avoid territoriality issues especially if you're keeping more than one rooster. It will also ensure that your pets or your flock are safe from outside predators, and harsh weather conditions. Durable housing is a must especially if you're keeping a show bird. They must have their own separate coops where they can freely roam around and see the outside without posing a threat to other roosters. You'll also learn about the location, size & the materials needed.

Housing Options for Roosters and Chickens

There are two main housing options for roosters, either you buy a coop or you build one yourself. If you choose to buy a ready made enclosure from a pet store or online, your options are usually a traditional wooden housing, and a plastic housing.

Wooden Housing

The main advantage of a wooden coop is that it's very strong and it can definitely withstand the weather conditions outside. When choosing a wooden coop, you want to make sure that the wood is made out of tanalized timber. A tanalized timber is the kind of wood that will not rot because it underwent pressure treatments that can lasts for a very long time.

Another important thing you need to consider aside from the wood is how the coop is built. You need to make sure that the housing is strong. You can do this by simply pushing it or shoving it so that you can feel if it's strong enough.

It's important that you look at how it was set up. You may want to get something that has a weld mesh instead of chicken wire especially in the run side of the coop. Weld mesh is really strong, and it has square holes in it. Never buy a cage that has chicken wire (hexagonal holes) in its run side because rats and other animals can easily break it. When it comes to security, you need to ensure that the coop you're getting has doors with strong bolts and hinges in it so that your rooster won't be able to escape.

If you're going to buy a wooden housing with a built - in nest box in it, you need to make sure that it has strong roosting bars (this is where chickens roost at night when they go to sleep) because they cling on to that, and can easily be broken if is not made out of timber or strong wood materials. The nest boxes should at least have 1 nest box for every 3 hens otherwise they could fight over it.

When getting a nest box separately, you would want something that can be easily detached so that you won't have a hard time cleaning it. Make sure to clean the coops at least once a week.

Generally, if you buy a ready made wooden coop, the house has two sides: the main house or the coop, and the run area where they can roam around in their own space but will still be able to see the outside without escaping from the enclosure. These are the two integral parts of the chicken enclosure. It's ideal that you allow at least one square meter of run space per chicken or rooster. Wooden housing costs more than plastic housing because the wood materials are strong and sturdy plus it depends on how well it was built, the brand, the size and the design of the enclosure. Prices range from around $500 and up.

Plastic Housing

There are also lots of keepers who choose to buy an enclosure made out of plastic and welded mesh for their chickens. This is because it's much cheaper, doesn't take up too much space, easy to wash, and also quite durable even if it is place outside. It usually looks like sort of a caged tent for your chickens. Another advantage is that plastic enclosures are usually less inclined to get mites compared to wooden housing, and it's very easy to clean, you can just jet wash it.

Plastic enclosures come in a variety of different designs, colors, and types. It usually has a run with strong welded mesh that is already attached with the plastic coop that can also be easily opened and clean. Some plastic cages also come with coop covers so that your pet is protected and they can still stroll within their run space during rainy days or hot weather. Your chicken won't like direct sunlight, and you shouldn't allow it too because it can dry up their skin. However, they'll still need a decent amount of light which is why coop covers are perfect. It can also protect them during windy days.

Chicken Arks

This is also made out of wood materials but it is mostly design for chicks and young chickens or juvenile ones. It's usually shaped like a triangular ark with a coop on one end, and a nesting box on the other as well as a run space in the middle that's also made out of welded mesh. A brooding hen is also perfect for such enclosures because it keeps them separate from the rest of the flocks allowing the moms to properly brood, and also protect chicks. It keeps the mother hen and her chicks isolated from the other chickens that could be annoying them (at least for the mean time). This type of enclosure is also lightweight but it has very strong construction, you can easily set it up or move it from one place to another.

Location and Size of the Enclosure

In terms of where to place your coop or chicken enclosures, you can place it in the grass if you have a garden or space in your backyard or you can also dig a shallow piece of land and place it on top of it. However, the most ideal location is to put it on top of a concrete base or a hard - standing base. You can easily renew the bedding underneath and it can be easily cleaned compared to when you place it on top of a soil/ground.

In terms of the size of the enclosure should of course depend on how big your rooster or chickens will get, and how many will stay inside it. Another general rule of thumb is that the more space, the better! If the housing or the space within the enclosure is limited, it can cause your rooster to be stressed out and could also become aggressive. You want to make sure that the run side of the enclosure has plenty of space so that they can still free range safely even if you're not around.

Chicken Bedding

Back in the day, keepers use straw but the problem with that is that the thin stalks accumulate bacteria and dust mites which can be harmful for your rooster in the long run. What you can do is buy horse bedding. It is a dry sort of stalks of hays that can be used in nest boxes, coops, and the run of your rooster's enclosure. The stalks are dry making it perfect for sucking the smell of their poops, and prevent a foul odor inside their enclosures. It's also environmentally friendly because once you replace it with new bedding; you can use the previous one and use it as a compost pit with your kitchen left overs at home.

Chapter Five: Nutrition and Feeding

Roosters just like any other household pets need the right nutrition in order to properly grow, maintain its health, and live a long life. Regardless whether you're keeping a rooster or a hen, you need to make sure that you'll provide them with basic nutrients that are of top quality including water. The water is oftentimes overlooked but it is necessary in order to ensure that the food you feed to your chickens is properly digested. Water can also help your rooster's longevity and maintain its physique. This chapter will provide you with the all the essential information you need about feeding your chickens, and your rooster in particular.

The Basics of Feeding a Chicken

Chickens in general are omnivores. Roosters and hens alike prefer feeding on various kinds of food, which is why you need to make sure that you give them a varied diet, and rotate their food options so that they won't be picky – eaters. You can do this by ensuring that you only purchase foods that are organic or a commercial feed that is of great quality. The supplements you'll provide them should also vary.

There are five basic components when it comes to feeding chickens; these are proteins, carbs, fats, vitamins and minerals. Such components will serve as the backbone of a healthy rooster. You need to ensure that the foods you feed your roosters contain most, if not all of these important components because it can benefit your roosters overall health, immune system, and physical appearance. Usually, lack of proper nutrition or lack of a missing food component can be shown through its dwindling health or sometimes its physique like the feathers, and skin. Sometimes it can affect the offspring as well during egg production (for hens), if the rooster is not healthy and does not receive proper nutrition it can affect the quality of the eggs.

Feeding a Rooster

The recommendations of what to feed a rooster greatly vary and most of the times confusing, this is because most roosters pretty much end up at the dinner table at a very young age. Hens are obviously more valuable than a rooster which is why if you ask breeders and even those who have flocks will tell you different things. There is no exact ratio of how much to feed a certain type of rooster, every single breed has its own taste and eating habit so you just have to find out for yourself what is best for your rooster as long as the five components are present, your rooster will be fine. However, there are some important things you need to know when feeding a rooster, one of which is that you shouldn't feed young male chicks or pullets with too much calcium enriched foods because it can cause damage in its kidneys. Too much calcium can also affect a rooster's ability to fertilize an egg. It's always best to ask a vet or its breeder at how much calcium is right for your rooster breed. In general, a rooster's diet should be high in protein and low in calcium.

Water for Your Roosters

As mentioned earlier, your rooster needs access to fresh and clean water all the time. The fresh water supply has many benefits for your chicken; one of the most important advantages is that if the rooster/chicken is properly dehydrated, it will eat the proper amount of food. If they don't drink a lot, chances are they won't also eat a lot. If you happen to own a laying hen, then fresh supply of water is definitely a must because it will help in producing the best quality of eggs (since eggs are mostly made with water). Never ever give dirty water to your pet rooster because it can cause digestive problems and other illnesses.

Feeding Scratch or Scraps to Your Roosters

All types of roosters (and hens) love to forage and dig around in the ground. They eat almost any type of insects, worms, grains and other things like pebbles, rodents, dirt etc. This is their natural instinct – to constantly dig around and chuckle to whatever they can find lying on the ground. In fact, chickens raised in environments that enable them to freely forage in the ground are much healthier and happier than those raised in coops filled with just commercial chicken feeds. If you don't have a foraging space in your backyard, then make sure that you buy a commercial scratch mixes so that they can practice this habit. If you want to go organic, you can feed them with scrap foods or leftovers like veggies, fruits, and the likes. Just make sure that these are also fresh and not rotten.

Feeding your roosters with chicken scraps either commercial ones or leftovers from your kitchen will serve as treats for them just like if you're feeding a parrot or similar types of bird species. Birds including chickens and roosters love treats because it's not just food for them; it's a form of exercise, and mental stimulation. Foraging keeps them entertained and it also helps in reducing kitchen waste!

Eating Habits of Roosters

It's important that you have knowledge of your pet's eating habits. You can observe it as they grow old if you're the one who'll raise it or you can ask the breeder about it. There are some breeds that will prefer a certain food brand, and will only eat a certain amount while there are those that would like to have more than enough. The eating habits of both roosters and hens are usually identical, but compared to hens, roosters will not need as much protein and calcium enriched foods because they're not going to lay eggs.

A rooster's main function especially in a flock is to fertilize the eggs, and also produce meat, if you wanted to produce a top quality meat, and a good supply of eggs, you have to ensure that the food you'll provide is a balanced and varied diet. There are lots of chicken feed brands that are already ready – made and also nutritionally balanced for almost any fowl species.

Perhaps the most noticeable eating habit of roosters is that they tend to be the one who finds the food source, and then call other chickens to partake in the meal. They usually guard the flock, and let the hens eat first before partaking. This is part of a rooster's natural instinct of being the provider and the 'watchdog.' There are other rooster species that are aggressive in nature, and will fight for a larger amount of food, if your rooster happens to be like that, then make sure to separate it from the flock at least during eating time.

In conclusion, the eating habit of your rooster depends on how it was raised, the amount you or the breeder usually feed, and also the type of rooster species you are raising.

Tips in Proper Feeding

- Roosters and chickens in general stop eating when they have already eaten the amount they need, make sure to fill their feeder dishes, and add more if need be or if they quickly consume it. If there's a lot of leftover, then just lessen the amount next time. This is how you can observe the eating habits of your rooster breed, and the amount of food it can consume.

- What most breeders do especially those who have a flock is buy a layer feed. You can also purchase a rooster bachelor pad so that you can feed your pet individually.

- If you own a flock, you can also just place the food in a raiser feed. Most keepers have observed that whenever they give their chickens with calcium enriched foods, the hens usually take what they need, and the roosters don't usually take interests in it.

- Make sure to provide fresh foods preferably organic so that they can maintain a good health. Never ever feed them with moldy or rotten foods because it can cause illnesses.

- There are no specific requirements for young chicks and fully – matured chickens, the nutrients are the same for both roosters and hens at any age. Do take note that you should feed less calcium to young pullets and roosters in general.

- Aside from commercial chicken feeds, kitchen scraps and the fresh dirt during foraging, you need to provide foods like cracked corns (for bantam rooster breeds), and whole corns (for regular rooster breeds). Meal worms can also be a supplement if your rooster doesn't have access to dirt or grass.

- It's best that you put the food in containers that are rodent proof especially at night.

- If you wanted to show your rooster or join a poultry showing competition, then you may need to provide an extra boost of nutrition to maintain its physique especially its plumage, and legs. Foods specific for showing birds can improve the color and quality of your pet's skin and feathers as well as improve its digestion making it more lean and noticeable with the judges.

Chapter Six: Grooming and Entertaining Your Roosters

This chapter will focus on how to groom your roosters and also keep them entertained! Aside from providing the right nutrition and the most comfortable enclosure for your newfound pet, it's also important that you keep them clean and happy! Sure it's hard to imagine how you can keep your fowl "clean" and well – groomed since they're always outside and, well, eating pretty much all the dirt in the ground, but cleaning them once in a while and making sure that their beaks are well – trimmed will maintain their overall health and hygiene. Keeping them entertained is also a good thing to do so that your roosters can stay occupied.

Grooming Your Roosters

Grooming your rooster isn't that hard, perhaps the only challenge you'll encounter when it comes to keeping them clean is how you handle them during the whole process so that they'll stay put and avoid any sort of mishap. There are two parts of rooster grooming; bathing and trimming. This section will teach on how to do just that!

Bathing Your Rooster

Bathing a rooster is not necessarily required but giving them a quick wash once in a while can be a good thing to ensure that they are in good condition. Generally, roosters cooperate during bath time (even the aggressive ones), just make sure that you know how to handle them properly. Here are some of the things you'll need in bathing your pet rooster:

- 2 Rubbermaid tubs (deep enough so that you can submerge your rooster)
- Lukewarm water (fill the tub until your rooster's neck)
- Mild soap or puppy soap/shampoo
- White Vinegar

- Towels
- Blow dryer
- Scrub Brush

How to Bathe a Rooster

Step #1: Get the supplies ready. Once you've prepared all the things you need to wash your rooster, then find a place where you can bathe your rooster (preferably outside). You can choose to do it in the morning or during hot weather.

Step #2: Add a small amount of mild soap in the tub. Once you've prepared the lukewarm water, you can then pour in a small amount of soap and let it bubble a bit.

Step #3: Place your rooster into the tub filled. Now that the tub is filled with bubbles and soap, you can slowly place your rooster in it. Make sure to hold him as he could flap his wings or try to escape. Just let him adjust to what's happening, he'll soon get used to it.

Step #4: Rub, rub, rub! Once your rooster has settled in, you can now gently rub the water with soap unto his body and feathers. Use your hands or finger tips when rubbing certain areas. Avoid letting the soap get in its eyes.

Step #5: Clean the dirtiest parts. The dirtiest parts of a rooster usually include the spots under the wings, areas around its vent, and of course it's feet and toenails. You can use a scrub brush in cleaning out the dirt under its feet or toenails.

Step #6: Rinse the rooster! You can let her bathe within a few minutes before rinsing. Once you are ready to rinse your rooster, slowly place her on the second tub filled with a little amount of vinegar (to remove the chemical residue of the soap). Begin to rinse him gently but still with a slightly tight grip. Avoid pouring water over his head or letting water run down its head. If there's soap around its head area just splash a bit of water over it until it's thoroughly rinsed.

Step #7: Dry your rooster with a soft towel. After thoroughly rinsing your pet, you can now wrap it with a soft towel and pat as much as you can to dry up the water accumulated in his feathers.

Step #8: Use a blow dryer to dry up its feathers. You would want to make sure that your rooster is all dried up before releasing it back to the flock. You can use a hair dryer to speed up the process and ensure that your rooster is all dried up (otherwise it can cause respiratory problems), make sure to only set the blow dryer to low and not too hot. And that's it!

The frequency of bathing your rooster is entirely up to you, it's best that you do this at least once or twice a month if you can or every other month. Don't overdo it because if you regularly bathe your chicken, it can dry up its skin and respiratory related illnesses (if they're not properly dried up). You should also make sure that you do it in a warm area so that your rooster won't catch a chill.

Bathing is also great way of also thoroughly examining your rooster if it's feathers, skin, feet, legs, and other body parts are in good condition. You would want to look out for any signs of mites, sores, feather patches, and feet problems especially during the blow drying process. This is also the time to check if its time to clip its toenails.

Trimming Your Rooster's Spurs

Trimming your rooster's spurs can be quite tricky especially if you don't know how to handle your rooster. You may want to get help to do this or better yet just go to a vet or a professional to do the trimming for your pet. This section will give you an overview on why you have to trim your rooster's spurs and how to do it yourself.

There are many reasons why people trim a chicken's spurs. This includes the following:

- Avoid injuries to hens during mating
- Avoid injuries to other roosters if ever cockfights break out
- Allows a rooster to walk easier

Cutting your rooster's spurs will not hurt them provided of course that you do it right. Basically there are two parts of a chicken's spurs; the inner core and the outer core. Just like a human fingernails, you just need to cut off the outer part or the hard skin, and avoid clipping the inner core to prevent bleeding. Here are some tips on how to properly clip your rooster's spurs:

- Hold your rooster upside down on its legs to fully grip it along with the spurs.
- Begin to cut the outer husk of your rooster's spur. You can use a plier to cut it smoothly.
- You can also twist off the spurs using the pliers but it can be quite hard.
- Make sure that you don't cut too close to the inner husk so that your chicken can still properly walk.
- You can also trim the toenails, just like clipping the spurs, just make sure that you don't cut the vein (usually the light colored nails) to avoid bleeding.

Entertaining Your Roosters

The Importance of Entertaining Your Roosters

Considering your rooster's quality of life is also important! Just like other household pets you need to provide your roosters with enough mental stimulation so that they'll avoid fighting with other chickens, and pretty much make their stay with you as happy as possible. As a matter of fact, chickens are can recognize animals and even people, this is why it's highly recommended that you spend time with them just like how you would with a dog or cat. Chickens who are stimulated are generally calmer pets compared to those who are not; those who are generally bored oftentimes became aggressive. Aggressive chickens especially roosters often attack those who are weak in the flock which can be stressful for both you and your other chickens. If you can provide them with toys to play with, you can keep aggression at bay.

Chickens love to belong in a flock, and rarely do they want to be alone, they tend to develop a social bond and hierarchy to species they spent time with. Playing with them and providing them with adequate toys is not just fun, it can also form a strong bond with you and your other pets.

How to Entertain Roosters

Some keepers who wanted to get creative, and also save money opt to just create their own chicken toys for their pet roosters especially while they're still young pullets. You can do a Do – It – Yourself toys to entertain your pets by following some recommendations below:

- **The Pecking Game**
  This is one of the simplest games you can provide for your rooster. If you want to take advantage of their pecking ability, you can do so by simply using an onion bag and hanging a cabbage that they can peck. As simple as it sounds, your roosters and hens will surely love it. This will sort of serve like their "punching bag."

- **Food Puzzle**
  Another simple game is a food puzzle. You just simply place a treat like a piece of fruit in a container where they need to figure out how to get it. An example is by simply putting a fruit in an ice block where you can freeze it. They'll have to constantly peck at it so that they can get the treat inside.

- **Chicken Gym**

  If you want to keep your roosters lean, then why not build a DIY chicken gym? All you need to do is to build a chicken swing out of a wooden frame and just attached it to a post. You can also build stages where they can climb up and down. This will surely keep their energies up!

- **Who's the fairest Chicken of them all?**

  Chickens in general are curious creatures, and they love shiny objects just like mirrors! Just place a small mirror (away from the sun's glare) in their pen to attract curios chicks and roosters.

There are a whole lot of DIY toy/game ideas for your roosters and hens alike. You can try different activities for them and get as creative as you can. As long as it's safe, imagination is the only limit!

Chicken Toys

If you don't have time to create a toy for your flock, then don't worry because you can purchase a lot of chicken toys from pet stores and online shops. This section will provide you with some of the most recommended toys to keep your rooster occupied.

- **Chick – N – Veggie Ball**

  This is a ready made version of the pecking game mentioned earlier. Here are some of its features:
    o It's easy to open
    o Can be quickly refilled
    o Has a sturdy and durable design
    o Can hold a cabbage, lettuce, broccolis and other similar sized veggies or fruits
    o Very easy to clean

- **Chicken Treat Ball**

  It's a ball where you can put small treats, and can also be hanged. It's usually made out of sturdy metal with large gaps of wiring enabling your chicken to easily get the food. It also comes with a bell making it more interesting for a curious cock. Here are some of its features:
    - The design of the ball caters to a rooster's foraging nature
    - It comes with a clip and hook where you can easily install anywhere
    - Includes a bell for added entertainment
    - Perfect for small treats
    - Has a quite challenging access to the food keeping them mentally stimulated

- **Lixit Chicken Toy**

  This is a branded toy for roosters and hens alike. It's sort of a feeder in a way because you can fill it with chicken feeds, worms/insects, and other treats that your pet likes. You may want to get more than one of these if you have many chickens so that they won't fight over it. Here are some key features:

  - It has an easy, pull apart and sturdy design
  - It can be rolled on the ground providing great entertainment for your flock
  - Can be filled with treats and kitchen scraps
  - Not meant for hanging

- **Chicken Swing**

  There are various designs of chicken swings that you can purchase in pet stores or online. These are the most popular toys in the market because chickens are very much delighted by it. It can also be used for pullets or young chicks, you can adjust the height as they grow, and watch them enjoy swinging. Some of the features include:

  o A durable and colorful toy
  o Roosters can easily perch on it
  o Has a perch size of around 16 inches.
  o Comes in many designs

Chapter Seven: Preparing Your Roosters for Show

Some people keep roosters for showing purposes, most often than not they already buy show quality birds and raise it so that the chicken can maintain its own set of unique qualities. If you wish to put your roosters on display, and possibly want to win a showing competition, then this chapter is for you! You will learn what it takes to raising show quality birds, and some guidelines you need to do before showing.

Tips in Preparing Your Roosters for Showing

There are a few things you need to keep in mind for you to ensure that the pullet you acquire is a show quality rooster. There are some regular breeds out there that are only use for its meat and to fertilize a hen's egg, while there are some that is bred for showing purposes. If showing is your main goal in keeping a pet rooster then make sure that you follow some of these tips below:

- **Acquire a show quality rooster from the best and reputable breeder.** As mentioned earlier, the best source for show quality birds are from private breeders. Never get a rooster from hatcheries or barnyard as well as farm stores because you won't be guaranteed that the bird is of top quality. Such breeders only care about the quantity of the chicks they produce more than its quality, and on top of that they usually don't know if the pullet is a male or a female! If the gender is not guaranteed, what more for the qualities of the breed?

- **Conduct a market research to find the most reputable breeders.** You shouldn't also just buy from private breeders, you need to conduct a bit of research of such breeder have done entered his existing flock of rooster collection for shows, and you need to interview the breeder thoroughly about the bird you're planning to get. Usually, you can find lots of local breeders that are selling their pullets for showing purposes, you would want to acquire a chick from somebody that has already an established reputation, or from someone that has acquired good feedback from previous clients. Make sure to check their breeding facilities, and see if the breeder's birds are NPIP certified along with other medical certifications. This will ensure that the breeder is legit, and that his collection of roosters are healthy and of top quality.

- **Select the right show breed.** Once you've picked your source, then it's time to select the rooster breed. Again, there are regular roosters, and there are those that is meant for show. Such roosters grow up to have a more colorful and lean physical appearance compared to ordinary ones. Of course, if the chick is still young, you won't be able to completely see its glory so you need to make sure that you ask the breeder if this is the right breed. You can also opt to contact first a local poultry group or show group if any to see if they can recommend a certain breeder that sells your breed of choice.

- **Be financially prepared.** Buying and raising show quality roosters do come with a price. Make sure that you are financially prepared if this is the path you wanted to take. The price tag for young pullets can be quite jaw – dropping especially if you're planning to acquire a rare breed. You also have to decide if the breed you're getting is already vaccinated, certified and the likes. The usual price for a rare rooster chick is around $50 and above (compared to regular breeds that only cost $3 on average). The rarer the breed, the more expensive it is. If you plan to acquire a more juvenile rooster and/or a fully – matured one, you'll definitely have to pay a lot more, perhaps the main advantage of doing so is that you can already see the "show qualities" of the bird. However, it's best that you acquire it as a young chick and be the one to raise them.

- **Maintain the quality of your show birds.** If you're planning to always show your roosters, and enter as many poultry competitions as you can, then it's a must that you maintain its health, and only care for a select number of breeds (preferably collect a few rooster with different sizes/colors). You need to ensure that you narrow down your roosters so that you can properly care for each breed. Ideally keeping 2 to 5 or more (if you can) show breeds is best if you wanted to maintain their qualities and your sanity as well! Most newbie fanciers keep at least 2 show birds so that they can compete in different poultry class

- **Developing the rooster and housing needs is essential.** There are three main factors that you need to follow in order to make sure that your roosters are fit for a competition. You have to ensure that you don't let your rooster breeds mix and don't let them socialize with the rest of the flock. Since your roosters are show birds, they need to be well – groomed and shouldn't have any scratches or missing feathers that can result if you let them mix in with other chickens. Remember, these are special birds, and for roosters it's quite inevitable that if you mix it with other roosters, it can wreak havoc in your collection. You can allow them to roam around your backyard to practice their "showing" skills, but don't let them stay with the rest of the flock.

- **Provide roosters with their own coops or enclosures.** Poultry birds should ideally be housed in their own coops or special enclosure that has enough room for them to move. If you have 2 or more show birds, you can buy a cage wherein it's separated but they can still see one another in order to provide companionship, and also avoid cockfights. Provide them with their own feeders/ water systems and litter areas as well.

- **Follow the standards of perfection for each of your rooster breed.** Each rooster has its own set of criteria that will be judged accordingly. If you wanted to win or at least let your roosters be among the top ranks, you need to ensure that you have prior knowledge with regards to its standard. The standard of perfection will vary; usually judges always favor birds with the best beak, shank, earlobe, and feather color. Other factors include its appropriate weight and size for its age, the keels, the condition of its feathers and the plumage, its health, and the rooster's temperament. As you join more showing competitions, you'll learn the tricks of the trade when it comes to prepping or selecting which rooster is fit for a show. Some 'show' birds who did not reach the "standards" are usually being culled and sometimes just being sold as quality pets or roosters to someone who doesn't intend to keep one for showing. Sometimes, they're being killed.

- **Attend a few bird shows before joining one.** Before taking the plunge or even considering buying a show bird, it's ideal that you attend a showing event first so that you'll know if this is something you wanted to do. Take the time to check out poultry shows around your area, talk to a couple of fanciers and show breeders, and learn as much as you can about the mechanics of showing.

- **Protect your rooster from diseases.** Showing birds are great but it also poses a threat to your rooster because if you let them join such contests, it can be exposed to different flocks and everything they carry, make sure that your rooster is healthy after the show, and maintained its hygiene and health.

Guidelines before Presenting Your Rooster

Before you present your rooster for show, make sure that you groomed them first so that they'll be at the best once judges see them. They should be clean, and their best physical characteristics should be highlighted if you wanted your rooster to stand out. Some owners pay much attention to their pet's feathers but forget that there are other factors. Here are some tips on how to groom and prepare your rooster for the show:

- **Get the supplies you need for grooming, and do a last minute "make – up session" before you present your rooster.** Some things you'll need include baby wipes, paper towels, comb, baby oil, nail polish, shine spray, spray bottle with water, VetRx, silk cloth, magic eraser and the likes. Of course, make sure that your chicken has taken a bath in your house before bringing them to the actual pet show.

- **Groom them up!** Once your grooming materials are ready, you can start to groom them starting from the top of its head down to its legs. You can use paper towels, magic eraser, and some baby wipes to remove dirt in your rooster's legs. You can also spray it with water to clean its legs and feet, after which apply a baby oil so that their legs will be shiny. You can also try to use a nail polish for its toenails.

- **Groom your rooster's comb.** In order for your pet's plumage or comb to pop and get noticed by the judges, you can apply baby oil and also put a VetRx in it. Don't let oil get into its feathers though. Taking good care of your rooster's comb is a must because this is one of your bird's best qualities so make sure to showcase it through proper grooming.

- **Fix the feathers if necessary.** Another thing you should focus on before presenting your bird is by fixing the fluff of their feathers. Use a s small comb to remove any dirt, and straighten out feathers in one direction so that it'll fluff nicely. You can use a silk cloth to make the feathers shiny or use a shine spray so that it'll wow the judges. Make sure to check for any twisted feathers, flatten them up as much as possible, and never try to pull a wing and tail feathers (since these are big feathers, it can be noticeable if pulled out).

- **Let your rooster shine!** After doing some finishing touches, you can then slowly place your pet inside its cage, head first so that the feathers won't get messed up. Run your fingers along its feathers to ensure that everything is straightened out. Finally, let your rooster just be himself, and dazzle the judges around!

Chapter Eight: Breeding Your Roosters

Breeding your chickens can be a lot of work especially for a newbie like you. There are a lot of things you need to learn if you wanted to produce the best eggs or simply raise hatchlings. It's also important to note that you need to have enough knowledge and time if you decided to breed chickens otherwise you might lose lots of eggs along the way. You also need to ensure that you have enough space in your backyard to accommodate the hatchlings as well as provide enough food for them during and after the breeding process so that they can produce the best possible offspring.

Time, effort, and money are needed if you wanted to breed chickens but it'll surely be a great learning experience if you do so. This chapter will provide you the basics of breeding chickens, how roosters mate with hens, how you can set up a breeding flock, and how to rear a hatchling.

How to Set Up the Breeding Flock

If you intend to use your chickens to have a steady supply of eggs that you can sell, or you wanted to raise your own breeds for show, then breeding your own flock is definitely what you should do because you can make sure that the chickens will be raised properly, and is of top quality. You and your family will surely enjoy the whole breeding process especially if you have kids, since chicks are very cute!

If you wanted to set up a flock, make sure that you have a healthy cock/rooster and hens. You can buy from reputable breeders, and set it up around spring time as this is the breeding season for chickens. However, before you build your flock, make sure that you have a breeding pen or have bought/build one. Your breeding flock should be separated from the rest of your chickens that you do not intend to breed. The breeding chickens should have their own separate enclosures, and the ratio of a rooster to hens should be 1:6 or 1:10 (1 rooster to 6 to 10 hens). Make sure that all hens and roosters within the flock are healthy and don't have any parasites, genetic problems, or infections. When you're all set, it's time to learn some breeding basics!

How Roosters Flirt with the Hens

Roosters don't just protect and provide food for their flock of hens; they also court them and flirt with them before mating. Just like other animals, chickens have their own way of mating rituals. As for roosters, what they do after spotting a hen that they like to mate with is to court them and flirt with them. The way they handle a particular hen will depend on the hen's personality, age, and breed. There are some roosters that are quite aggressive and will tend to skip the courting stage, and just go directly with mating the hens by chasing them; this is usually where hens get injured.

Part of the courting ritual involves the rooster constantly out with his selected hen/s, you'll notice that he will accompany her during feeding time, foraging, and hunting food source. The rooster will usually grab a worm or insect for the hens to let her know that he can provide for her needs if they stay close to him. In fact, when a rooster likes a hen, what he does is sort of impress the hen by showing off his wings and flaunt its awesome plumage.

Sometime they do a chicken hug wherein he will flap its arm or wings around the hen.

Roosters also tend to get territorial, if they see another rooster lurking around in his flock that's where cockfights usually happen. They'll fight to the death as if they're fighting a predator just so they can keep their hens, and rule the flock. This is the reason why every rooster you add in your flock should have their own corresponding hens.

If you happen to have only one rooster and a hen, make sure that you let the hen rest everyday for a few hours by separating them so that she won't be exhausted because of the mating process especially if you have quite an aggressive rooster.

The Mating Process

Once the rooster caught the hen's attention, and the hen is ready to mate, she'll squat for the rooster and let him mount her. It usually takes just about a minute or less to mate but some roosters do it much longer. There are some roosters that are quite aggressive during mating causing injuries and loss of feathers especially at the back of her neck and other parts of their bodies. This is why clipping your rooster's toenails is good so that it can prevent further injuries and feather plucking to your hen during mating. You can also try to buy poultry saddles to protect the hens. Usually, roosters mate with many hens in a day.

The act of mating is also called treading, this happens when a rooster and a hen's sexual organ (also known as papilla) touches; sometimes it's also known as the cloacal kiss. The rooster's papilla can be found inside his vent.

There are hens that refuse to mate with a rooster even if the rooster had done the courting ritual. When this happens, roosters will get upset but will still try to get the hen one way or another usually this is where chasing happens.

As mentioned earlier, hens do need to take a break from mating with your rooster. This is because too much mating can cause stress to the hem (especially if she's not in the mood), and can get the eggs stuck inside of her.

Egg Fertilization

Once your hen laid eggs, you need to regularly collect it, so that you can choose which eggs to brood. Some breeders suggest that you store the eggs for about 24 hours before incubating it to ensure successful hatching. Eggs will not become embryos without undergoing the incubation process. Here are some tips when collecting and storing the eggs for incubation:

- Make sure that you have clean hands so that you won't pass on any possible pathogens into the porous shell of the eggs.
- Be very careful in handling the eggs, and don't break it.
- Clean the nest and ensure that it is free of any muds or dirt to keep the fertilized eggs clean; otherwise you need to clean it up before incubation using sanitizer and lukewarm water.
- Whenever you're selecting an egg to hatch, pick out the eggs with a regular shape, and those that has no cracks whatsoever.
- You can store the fertilized eggs for up to seven days before incubating it. Make sure to store it in a place with high humidity and with a temperature of just 13 degrees Celsius.
- Turn or tilt the eggs once in a while so that the inner membrane won't be stuck on its outer shell.

Egg Hatching

There are two options to incubate the eggs, you either use your brooding hen or buy an incubator. Of course, incubators are more reliable but you need to make sure that you keep an eye out so as not to overdo it.

Letting your hen incubate her eggs is also good but maybe not ideal especially if you want to produce top quality eggs. If you choose to incubate the eggs through brooding, ensure that your hen has its own brooding area or nesting box. You can buy a rabbit hutch if you like because it gives the option of a quiet area where your hen can peacefully do its nesting. It should be separate to its feeders and water supply, and the nesting area should also be humid.

Big mother hens can incubate up to 12 eggs, while smaller ones can fully incubate up to 6 eggs only. Make sure that all the eggs are fully covered so that it's incubated to completion. It usually takes 21 days before the eggs will start to hatch, the incubation period may vary from one breed to another. Once the eggs hatch, she'll leave the nest, and it's now your job to dispose any eggs that were not hatched.

Chick Rearing

Once the chicks come out, make sure that they are separated from the hens and your whole flock until they are around six weeks old. Keep them in their nesting area for 1 week or so until they can handle the temperature outside. Once they're ready to come outside, make sure that they are properly secure to avoid being snatched by a predator or escaping. You can now introduce them to the rest of the flock, but don't worry about it because their mother hen will protect them from other chickens if need be. If you think they are in danger from your other collection, then separate them for the mean time until they're bigger before reintroducing them to the flock. The mother hen will usually teach their chicks everything they need to know, your job is to just provide adequate food and water for them as well as the right housing environment so that they'll grow right.

Caponizing or Neutering Roosters

Caponizing or neutering a rooster means removing its sexual organ or its testicle to prevent unwanted pregnancy. If your rooster is caponized, it will eliminate the production of testosterone in its body changing the way it acts with the opposite sex, becomes less aggressive with other roosters, and also lose interest in mating. Some keepers who raise roosters for its meat tend to neuter their breeds because the fowl rapidly gain weight, and also makes the meat taste a little less stringy. It is important to note that neutering a rooster is a delicate process, don't attempt to do this yourself if you're not an expert because it can be dangerous for your pet.

Guidelines in Caponizing a Rooster

For you to have an idea of the neuter process, we'll give you some guidelines in this section. Again, it is ideal that you ask help from an expert if you wanted your rooster to be caponized.

- Clean your pet rooster with soap and water. Make sure that you thoroughly rinse it to avoid any sort of soap residue.

- Ensure that all the surgical tools you're going to use are clean and sterilized otherwise it can infect your rooster.

- Prepare to make an incision or a cut. You should cut about 1 inch long at the bottom of your rooster's ribs. Usually, vets and professionals will use surgical rib spreaders in order to keep the cut or incision open.

- Once it is full open, you can then locate your rooster's testicle which is a small oval shape that is color yellow. Vets usually use tweezers to locate the testicles, and also move the tissues of the rooster. Once you find your rooster's testicles, you can now gently remove it.

- After removing the organ, you can then close the wound, and clean the incision using iodine.

- Vets will then stitched up the incision using sterile materials. Ensure that you will leave no foreign objects or feathers inside before stitching it up.

- After performing the operation, you need to isolate your rooster from the rest of the flock to ensure that the wound will not get infected, and not be scratched or harmed by other birds.

- Most vets will advise you to check the incision at least 2x a day to ensure that there's no infection. You can expect the wound to heal after a few days.

- It's ideal that you use a dissolvable kind of stiches or request it to your vet because you don't have to remove it once the wound has completely healed. Otherwise you'll need to remove the thread about a week or so after the surgery.

- Neutering a rooster yourself is not recommended unless you are an expert or have previously performed such surgery, it's better to bring your pet to the veterinarian and let the doctors handle it. This guide is only outlined to give you an overview about the neutering process.

Chapter Nine: Keeping Your Roosters Healthy

Roosters and chickens in general are prone to many bird illnesses which is why it's important that you have knowledge about the possible diseases that your rooster may acquire while you're raising it. There are some diseases that can affect and damage your bird's health and physical appearance, and can even be fatal for them while there are minor illnesses that can be easily prevented and treated. The key to making sure that your rooster is healthy and protected is to keep its housing environment clean, follow proper husbandry practices, feed it with the right nutrition, and keep it vaccinated and bring it to the vet once in a while for a routine check – up to ensure that your pet is at its prime health.

This chapter will cover all the most common illnesses acquired by chickens, their nature, causes, treatment, and the vaccines needed to prevent such diseases from affecting your pet's health. Keeping your roosters healthy is a must especially if you're planning to use it for showing, for fertilizing eggs, and even for using its meat.

Common Avian Illnesses

Usually diseases are more common when you're keeping a flock because it can quickly spread from one bird to another, so make sure that you pay enough attention to each of your fowl and their health to prevent the spread of unwanted diseases. Acquiring a serious or possibly fatal illness is highly unlikely especially if your pets are well vaccinated and if you follow proper husbandry practices. It's still good to have knowledge about the common avian diseases so that you'll know what to do in case your birds acquire one. This section will cover the symptoms, causes, and treatments as well the vaccines you need to prevent it.

- **Avian/ Chicken Pox**

  A chicken pox is usually transmitted virally or through mosquitoes. It is usually acquired from other chickens or roosters exhibiting the disease. It can affect a young pullet and fully – matured roosters. Symptoms of chicken pox include white spots on its skin, scabby sores that form in its comb/plumage, and a white pus in the mouth area or on its trachea. The usual treatment is to give a soft food during the condition, and provide a humid environment. This is a very common illness that can be easily treated; just make sure to separate your rooster from the flock to avoid passing the disease. Those birds that have already experienced the disease are already immune from it.

- **Chicken Cholera**

  Cholera is a bacterial disease that can also be transmitted from one rooster to another or through the feces of animals like rats, birds, raccoons, contaminated soil, and unclean water or feeder. The usual symptoms include yellowish or greenish diarrhea, darkened comb and wattles, swollen joints, and difficulty in breathing. It usually affects roosters over 4 months of age. It doesn't affect humans but unfortunately this is a fatal disease. There's no treatment for chicken cholera, if you find out that your pet acquired one, you have no choice but to kill it or just let it die otherwise it will definitely be a carrier (even if it recovers) and could infect your flock. You can avail a vaccine being administered by the Department of Agriculture or a similar organization in your state/country.

- **Bronchitis**

  Another common viral disease that is highly contagious is bronchitis. It can quickly spread through contact, airborne, and contaminated materials. Symptoms include coughing, discharge from its eyes and nose as well as sneezing or difficulty in breathing. It can be easily treated through supportive care, but if the chicks that is 6 weeks and below acquired it, it can be fatal. Vaccines are usually given at a young age.

- **Mareks Disease**

  This is one of the most fatal diseases that your rooster can acquire. It usually affects chickens that are 20 weeks old and below. It's a viral disease that can easily spread to other fowls if they inhale a skin cell or a feather dust of an infected bird. Symptoms include paralysis, external and internal tumors, and no reaction to light because it turns the iris of the eye to gray or dull color. Unfortunately, there's no treatment for this disease, there's a high death rate among chickens once they acquire it, and even if they survived they will become carriers. Vaccines are given to one day old chicks.

- **Moniliasis**

  This is a fungal disease that is usually acquired in feeders with molds or water dishes that are contaminated with carriers. Symptoms include white pus or a cheesy material in crop, inflammation of the vent, ruffled feathers, and a droopy looking physique. It can be treated using an antifungal medication called Nystatin. There is no vaccination available to prevent this, the best you can for prevention is to sanitize the feeders and water dishes, and make sure that other birds are not carriers.

- **Omphalitis**

  It is another bacterial infection affecting the naval that is usually contracted from unclean or unsanitary enclosures or surfaces. It mostly affects chicks that are a few weeks old especially those who have weak immune systems. Symptoms include inflamed, enlarged and bluish - colored naval area, drowsy chicks, and bad smelling chicks. Antibiotics are use to treat omphalitis in chicks, some chicks can die but most will recover as long as the coops or enclosures are clean. There is no vaccine to prevent this, but it's important to note that it can infect humans. Be careful and take precautionary measures whenever your handling infected birds.

- **Coccidiosis**

  This is a parasitic condition in which the parasites (which has 6 kinds of species) damage the gut walls of your rooster or chicken. The different species or parasites that cause Coccidiosis have varying effects that can be life – threatening for your pet. When the gut walls is damaged there bacteria used for digestion will be disrupted and will allow the harmful ones to take over which can eventually lead to blood poisoning. Symptoms include loss of appetite, blood in the feces, dehydration, pale wattles and plumage, droopiness, and shakiness. Most chickens don't survive this illness, but treatments are available. Your vet may recommend an anticoccidial type of medication to control the harmful bacteria. Other forms of antibiotics are usually given. You'll also be advised to provide your pet with a warm, clean and dry environment followed with multivitamins intake or a probiotic.

Chapter Ten: Care Sheet and Summary

Before this book comes to an end, this chapter will highlight all of the most important things you need know from each chapter so that you can easily have a quick look if you need information on the go. I hope you enjoyed reading this book, and have learned a lot in terms of keeping a rooster. Now it's time to apply the knowledge you learned, we hope you become a reputable rooster breeder!

General Information

- **Taxonomy:** Kingdom Animalia, Phylum Chordata, Class Aves, Order Galliformes, Family Phasianidae, Genus Gallus, and Species Gallus gallus.
- **Distribution:** Mostly distributed in different countries in Asia such as India, Philippines, China, Indonesia, Malaysia, and Burma
- **Size:** Roosters on average has a length of 25 to 40 centimeters
- **Weight:** Domestic rooster chickens weighs about 8 ½ pounds (around 3 kg) on average
- **Wingspan:** Roosters on average has a wingspan that measures about 60 to 90 centimeters.
- **Lifespan:** The average lifespan of a rooster is 5 to 7 years but there have been instances where they live for more than 10 years

Keeping Roosters as Pets

Acquiring a Rooster Permit

- Know your jurisdiction.
- Inquire in your local government about the regulations regarding poultry keeping.
- Search online regarding the laws
- Visit your local courthouse

- Talk to your local associations or subdivision organizations

Rooster Regulations You May Encounter

- Licensing/Permit Fees
- Number of Birds You Can Legally Keep
- Rooster Regulations
- Housing Requirements
- Public Concerns
- Rooster Slaughtering
- Special Regulations

Costs of Keeping a Rooster

- Purchase Price: for Ordinary roosters: $3 to $5; for hybrid roosters: $30 to $50 and above per chick.
- Housing Expenses: $500 - $1,000 to $4,000
- Feeders/Dishes: $8 to $40
- Bedding: $3 to $12 per 40 pounds of bag
- Food Expenses: $15 to $20 per 50 pounds of bag
- Miscellaneous Expenses: $10 to $100

How to Purchase and Select a Healthy Rooster

Where to Purchase Roosters

- Farm Stores
- Chick Hatchery
- Private/Backyard Breeders
- Adoption Centers

Guidelines before Purchasing a Rooster

These are some questions you need to ask a breeder and yourself before buying a chick include the following:

- What rooster breeds are available?
- Can I purchase sexed chickens?
- Is the breeder NPIP (National Poultry Improvement Plan) Certified?
- What is the heritage of the roosters?
- How old is the chick?
- What's the personality of the rooster breed?
- Is the chick or rooster vaccinated already?
- What are the environmental restrictions for the specific rooster breed?
- What do they feed on?
- Is your place safe from predators?
- Is the breed suitable for you?

Coops and Enclosures for Roosters

Guidelines When Buying a Rooster Coop/Enclosure:

Wooden Housing

- You want to make sure that the wood is made out of tanalized timber.
- You need to make sure that the housing is strong.
- It's important that you look at how it was set up. You may want to get something that has a weld mesh instead of chicken wire especially in the run side of the coop.
- When it comes to security, you need to ensure that the coop you're getting has doors with strong bolts and hinges in it so that your rooster won't be able to escape.

Nesting Box

- If you're going to buy a wooden housing with a built - in nest box in it, you need to make sure that it has strong roosting bars.
- The nest boxes should at least have 1 nest box for every 3 hens otherwise they could fight over it.
- When getting a nest box separately, you would want something that can be easily detached so that you won't have a hard time cleaning it.

- Make sure to clean the coops at least once a week.

Plastic Housing

- It should be cheaper.
- It shouldn't take up too much space.
- It should be easy to wash.
- Should be durable and strong even if it is place outside.
- The run part of the enclosure should be made out of a strong welded mesh that is already attached with the plastic coop so that it can be easily opened and clean.

Chicken Arks

- This type of enclosure should be lightweight.
- It should have a very strong construction.
- It should be easy to set up or move it from one place to another.

Nutrition and Feeding

The Basics of Feeding a Chicken

- Chickens in general are omnivores.

- There are five basic components when it comes to feeding chickens; these are proteins, carbs, fats, vitamins and minerals.
- You shouldn't feed young male chicks or pullets with too much calcium enriched foods because it can cause damage in its kidneys. Too much calcium can also affect a rooster's ability to fertilize an egg.
- They eat almost any type of insects, worms, grains and other things like pebbles, rodents, dirt aside from commercial chicken feeds
- If you want to go organic, you can feed them with scrap foods or leftovers like veggies, fruits, and the likes.

Grooming and Entertaining Your Roosters

How to Bathe a Rooster

Step #1: Get the supplies ready.

Step #2: Add a small amount of mild soap in the tub.

Step #3: Place your rooster into the tub filled.

Step #4: Rub, rub, rub!

Step #5: Clean the dirtiest parts.

Step #6: Rinse the rooster!

Step #7: Dry your rooster with a soft towel.

Step #8: Use a blow dryer to dry up its feathers.

How to Entertain Roosters

You can do a Do – It – Yourself toys to entertain your pets by following some recommendations below:

- The Pecking Game
- Food Puzzle
- Chicken Gym

Tips in Preparing Your Roosters for Show

- Acquire a show quality rooster from the best and reputable breeder.
- Conduct a market research to find the most reputable breeders.
- Select the right show breed.
- Be financially prepared.
- Maintain the quality of your show birds.
- Developing the rooster and housing needs is essential.
- Provide roosters with their own coops or enclosures.
- Follow the standards of perfection for each of your rooster breed.

- Attend a few bird shows before joining one.
- Protect your rooster from diseases.

Breeding Your Roosters

The Mating Process

- Once the rooster caught the hen's attention, and the hen is ready to mate, she'll squat for the rooster and let him mount her.
- It usually takes just about a minute or less to mate but some roosters do it much longer.
- The act of mating is also called treading, this happens when a rooster and a hen's sexual organ (also known as papilla) touches; sometimes it's also known as the cloacal kiss.

Egg Fertilization

- You can store the fertilized eggs for up to seven days before incubating it. Make sure to store it in a place with high humidity and with a temperature of just 13 degrees Celsius.

Egg Hatching

- Big mother hens can incubate up to 12 eggs, while smaller ones can fully incubate up to 6 eggs only.
- It usually takes 21 days before the eggs will start to hatch, the incubation period may vary from one breed to another.

Common Illnesses of Roosters

- Avian/ Chicken Pox
- Chicken Cholera
- Bronchitis
- Mareks Disease
- Moniliasis
- Omphalitis
- Coccidiosis

Photo Credits

Page 1 Photo by user Pexels via Pixabay.com, https://pixabay.com/en/animal-avian-bird-feathers-macro-1867562/

Page 5 Photo by user Momentmal via Pixabay.com, https://pixabay.com/en/hahn-feather-close-poultry-pride-2845277/

Page 19 Photo by user Pexels via Pixabay.com, https://pixabay.com/en/rooster-cock-chicken-foul-farm-1284283/

Page 35 Photo by user Momentmal via Pixabay.com, https://pixabay.com/en/hahn-feather-close-poultry-pride-2847352/

Page 49 Photo by user j_a_uppendahl via Pixabay.com, https://pixabay.com/en/alive-black-chicken-hen-farm-bird-2358942/

Page 56 Photo by user Irina_kukuts via Pixabay.com, https://pixabay.com/en/cock-bird-village-animal-poultry-2525749/

Page 65 Photo by user Angela Quinn via Pixabay.com, https://pixabay.com/en/rooster-chicken-hen-peck-farming-1001892/

Page 77 Photo by user Pexels via Pixabay.com, https://pixabay.com/en/rooster-nature-outdoors-bird-1839644/

Page 87 Photo by user ttcteam via Pixabay.com, https://pixabay.com/en/trapped-chicken-cage-rooster-2400698/

Page 99 Photo by user ugglemamma via Pixabay.com, https://pixabay.com/en/rooster-walk-trudging-step-2498527/

Page 106 Photo by user CandiceJax via Pixabay.com, https://pixabay.com/en/rooster-chicken-farm-hen-bird-2832520/

References

"5 Important Tips on Raising Roosters" -
RuralLivingToday.com
https://rurallivingtoday.com/backyard-chickens-roosters/5-
important-tips-raising-roosters/

"7 Ways To Prevent Worm Infestations In Your Chickens"
- ChickenHeavenOnEarth.com
https://www.chickenheavenonearth.com/7-ways-to-prevent-
worms-from-infesting-your-chickens-chicken-heaven-on-
earth.html

"Are You Wondering What Do Roosters Eat?" -
CountrySideNetwork.com
https://countrysidenetwork.com/daily/poultry/feed-
health/are-you-wondering-what-do-roosters-eat/

**"Best Chicken Toys: Entertaining Your Backyard
Chickens"** - RuralLivingToday.com
https://rurallivingtoday.com/backyard-chickens-
roosters/best-chicken-toys-entertaining-your-backyard-
chickens/

"Chickens" - Animal Corner UK
https://animalcorner.co.uk/animals/chickens/

"Chickens" - Wikipedia.org
https://en.wikipedia.org/wiki/Chicken

"Chicken Bath 101" - CommunityChickens.com
https://www.communitychickens.com/chicken-bath-101/

"Chicken Laws and Ordinances: Is It Legal To Keep
Chickens Where You Live?"- BackYardChickens.com
https://www.backyardchickens.com/articles/chicken-laws-
and-ordinances-and-how-to-change-them.65675/

"Different Kinds of Roosters" - Roysfarm.com
http://www.roysfarm.com/different-kinds-of-roosters/

"Eating Habits of Chickens & Roosters" - Roysfarm.com
http://www.roysfarm.com/eating-habits-of-chickens-
roosters/

"Gallus gallus, chicken" - GeoChemBio.com
http://www.geochembio.com/biology/organisms/chicken/

"How Many Roosters Should I Buy?" -
MailOrderPoultry.com
https://www.mailorderpoultry.com/how-many-roosters-
should-i-buy/

"How To Caponize A Chicken" -
ChickenHeavenOnEarth.com
https://www.chickenheavenonearth.com/how-to-caponizeneuter-a-roosters-chicken-heaven-on-earth.html

"How To Keep Rooster's Quiet" -
ChickenHeavenOnEarth.com
https://www.chickenheavenonearth.com/how-to-keep-roosters-quiet-rooster-no-crow-collars--more-tips.html

"How to Remove Rooster Spurs" - FowlVisions.com
http://www.fowlvisions.com/how-to-remove-rooster-spurs/

"How To Introduce A Rooster Into Your Flock" -
ChickenHeavenOnEarth.com
https://www.chickenheavenonearth.com/how-to-introduce-a-rooster-into-your-flock-of-hens-chicken-heaven-on-earth.html

"It's showtime! The judges are ready, are your chickens ready?" - PoultryShowCentral.com
https://www.poultryshowcentral.com/grooming-for-show.html

"Pros and Cons of Keeping a Rooster ~ Learn Which is Best for You" - RuralLivingToday.com
https://rurallivingtoday.com/backyard-chickens-roosters/pros-cons-keeping-rooster/

"Raising Show Chickens" - HobbyFarms.com
http://www.hobbyfarms.com/raising-show-chickens/

"Rooster" - Wikipedia.org
https://en.wikipedia.org/wiki/Rooster

"Rooster Mating & Courting Rituals: How Rooster's Act With Hens" - ChickenHeavenOnEarth.com
https://www.chickenheavenonearth.com/rooster-mating-rituals.html

"Trimming Chickens Spurs & Toenails" - Ultimate Fowl
https://ultimatefowl.wordpress.com/2009/06/16/199/

"Types Of Worms That Infest Chickens & How To Stop Them" - ChickenHeavenOnEarth.com
https://www.chickenheavenonearth.com/types-of-worms-that-infest-chickens--how-to-stop-them-chicken-heaven-on-earth.html

"Will My Council Allow Me To Keep Chickens?" -
BackYardChickenCoops.com
https://www.backyardchickencoops.com.au/will-my-
council-allow-me-to-keep-chickens

Feeding Baby
Cynthia Cherry
978-1941070000

Axolotl
Lolly Brown
978-0989658430

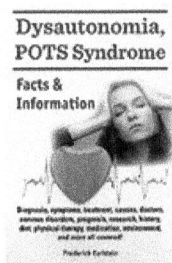

Dysautonomia, POTS
Syndrome
Frederick Earlstein
978-0989658485

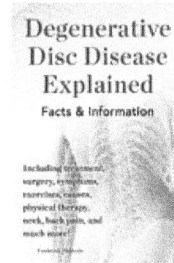

Degenerative Disc
Disease Explained
Frederick Earlstein
978-0989658485

Sinusitis, Hay Fever,
Allergic Rhinitis Explained
Frederick Earlstein
978-1941070024

Wicca
Riley Star
978-1941070130

Zombie Apocalypse
Rex Cutty
978-1941070154

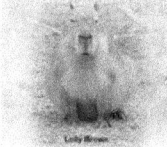

Capybara
Lolly Brown
978-1941070062

Eels As Pets
Lolly Brown
978-1941070167

Scabies and Lice Explained
Frederick Earlstein
978-1941070017

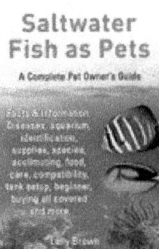

Saltwater Fish As Pets
Lolly Brown
978-0989658461

Torticollis Explained
Frederick Earlstein
978-1941070055

Kennel Cough
Lolly Brown
978-0989658409

Physiotherapist, Physical
Therapist
Christopher Wright
978-0989658492

Rats, Mice, and Dormice
As Pets
Lolly Brown
978-1941070079

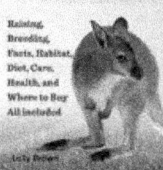

Wallaby and Wallaroo Care
Lolly Brown
978-1941070031

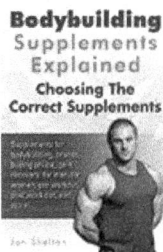

Bodybuilding Supplements
Explained
Jon Shelton
978-1941070239

Demonology
Riley Star
978-19401070314

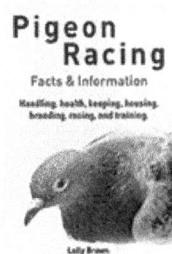

Pigeon Racing
Lolly Brown
978-1941070307

Dwarf Hamster
Lolly Brown
978-1941070390

Cryptozoology
Rex Cutty
978-1941070406

Eye Strain
Frederick Earlstein
978-1941070369

Inez The Miniature Elephant
Asher Ray
978-1941070353

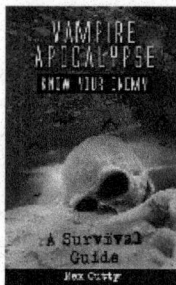

Vampire Apocalypse
Rex Cutty
978-1941070321

www.ingramcontent.com/pod-product-compliance
Lightning Source LLC
Chambersburg PA
CBHW052109090426
42741CB00009B/1745